NFL TODAY

THE STORY OF THE

MIAMI DOLPHINS

THE STORY OF THE MIAMI DOLPHINS

JIM WHITING

CREATIVE EDUCATION

PUBLISHED BY CREATIVE EDUCATION
P.O. BOX 227, MANKATO, MINNESOTA 56002
CREATIVE EDUCATION IS AN IMPRINT OF THE CREATIVE COMPANY
WWW.THECREATIVECOMPANY.US

DESIGN AND PRODUCTION BY BLUE DESIGN
ART DIRECTION BY RITA MARSHALL
PRINTED IN THE UNITED STATES OF AMERICA

PHOTOGRAPHS BY CORBIS (ATLANTIDE
PHOTOTRAVEL, VICK MCKENZIE/NEWSPORT), GETTY
IMAGES (DOUG BENC, BRUCE BENNETT STUDIOS,
GEORGE GOJKOVICH, SAM GREENWOOD, ROD HANNA/
NFL, WALTER IOOSS JR./SPORTS ILLUSTRATED, ALLEN
KEE, KIDWILER COLLECTION/DIAMOND IMAGES,
STREETER LECKA, NEIL LEIFER/SPORTS ILLUSTRATED,
GEORGE LONG/NFL, TAKASHI MAKITA/NFL, NFL,
RONALD MARTINEZ, RONALD MARTINEZ/ALLSPORT,
AL MESSERSCHMIDT/NFL, RONALD C. MODRA/SPORTS
IMAGERY, DARRYL NORENBERG/NFL, JC RIDLEY/NFL,
GEORGE ROSE, MANNY RUBIO/NFL, MARK SEROTA,
GEORGE TIEDEMANN/SPORTS ILLUSTRATED, WINSLOW
TOWNSON, RHONA WISE/AFP)

LIBRARY OF CONGRESS CATALOGING-IN-PUBLICATION DATA
WHITING, JIM.
THE STORY OF THE MIAMI DOLPHINS / BY JIM WHITING.
P. CM. — (NFL TODAY)
INCLUDES INDEX.
SUMMARY: THE HISTORY OF THE NATIONAL FOOTBALL LEAGUE'S
MIAMI DOLPHINS, SURVEYING THE FRANCHISE'S BIGGEST STARS
AND MOST MEMORABLE MOMENTS FROM ITS INAUGURAL SEASON
IN 1966 TO TODAY.
ISBN 978-1-60818-308-1
1. MIAMI DOLPHINS (FOOTBALL TEAM)—HISTORY—JUVENILE
LITERATURE. I. TITLE.

GV956.M47W55 2013
796.332'6409759381—DC23   2012031648

FIRST EDITION
9 8 7 6 5 4 3 2 1

COVER: QUARTERBACK RYAN TANNEHILL
PAGE 2: NOSE TACKLE BOB BAUMHOWER
PAGES 4—5: RUNNING BACK LARRY CSONKA
PAGE 6: RUNNING BACK PATRICK COBBS (TOP) AND OFFENSIVE
TACKLE JAKE LONG

TABLE OF CONTENTS

SIDELINE STORIES

MEET THE DOLPHINS

Football Down South

Most people associate Florida with year-round sunshine, white sandy beaches, and tropical temperatures. Yet it was a rare cold snap that helped bring about the creation of Miami, the state's largest city. In the winter of 1894–95, back-to-back freezes in central and northern Florida destroyed citrus-tree plantations and wiped out many fortunes. Julia Tuttle, a widow who owned 640 acres on the site of present-day Miami, told railroad mogul Henry Flagler that her crops had escaped the frost. She offered to swap some of her land in exchange for extending his tracks to her property and starting a town. Today, a little more than a century later, Miami and its surrounding area has become a major metropolis that ranks seventh in population among all United States cities.

Seventy years after Flagler's trains began rumbling into Miami, Minnesota attorney Joe Robbie put the city on track for a franchise in the upstart American Football League (AFL). One of Robbie's clients wanted a franchise in the new league, which had just

DEFENSIVE TACKLE MANNY FERNANDEZ DOMINATED IN MIAMI'S FIRST SUPER BOWL WIN

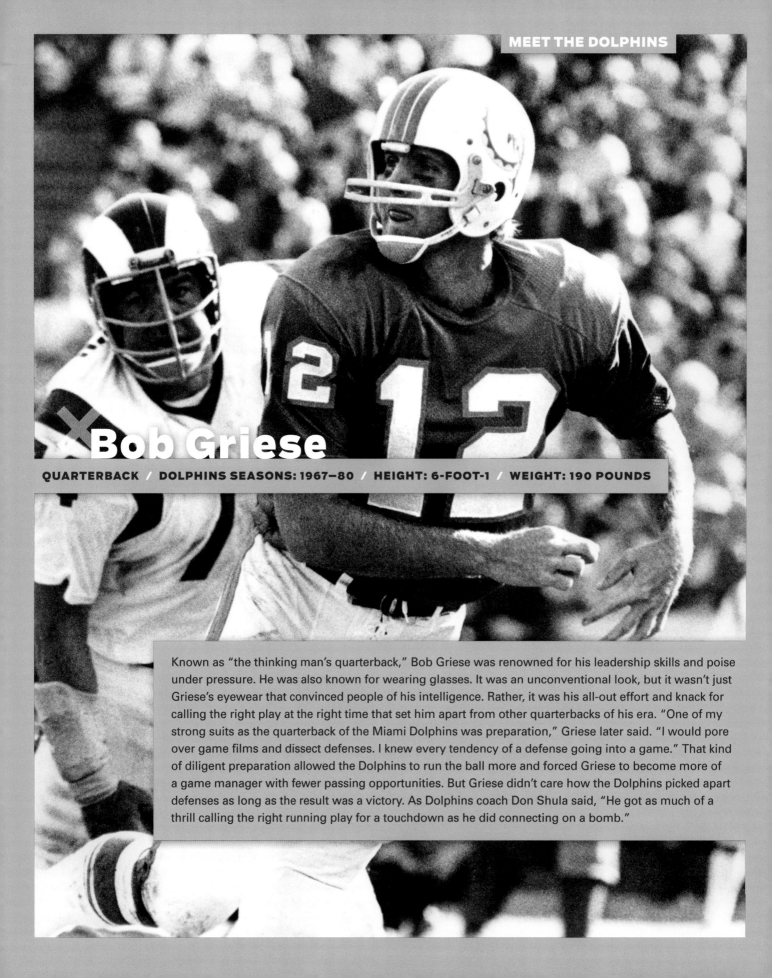

Bob Griese

QUARTERBACK / DOLPHINS SEASONS: 1967–80 / HEIGHT: 6-FOOT-1 / WEIGHT: 190 POUNDS

Known as "the thinking man's quarterback," Bob Griese was renowned for his leadership skills and poise under pressure. He was also known for wearing glasses. It was an unconventional look, but it wasn't just Griese's eyewear that convinced people of his intelligence. Rather, it was his all-out effort and knack for calling the right play at the right time that set him apart from other quarterbacks of his era. "One of my strong suits as the quarterback of the Miami Dolphins was preparation," Griese later said. "I would pore over game films and dissect defenses. I knew every tendency of a defense going into a game." That kind of diligent preparation allowed the Dolphins to run the ball more and forced Griese to become more of a game manager with fewer passing opportunities. But Griese didn't care how the Dolphins picked apart defenses as long as the result was a victory. As Dolphins coach Don Shula said, "He got as much of a thrill calling the right running play for a touchdown as he did connecting on a bomb."

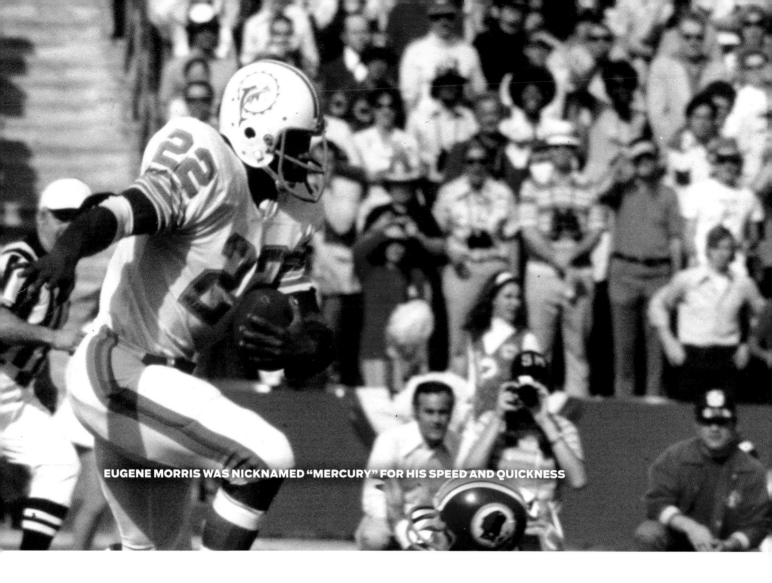

EUGENE MORRIS WAS NICKNAMED "MERCURY" FOR HIS SPEED AND QUICKNESS

emerged as a rival to the long-established National Football League (NFL). Robbie and AFL commissioner Joe Foss had been classmates and friends at the University of South Dakota. Foss wanted a team in Miami. Robbie's client wasn't interested in that location, but Robbie was, and he joined with actor and entertainer Danny Thomas to establish a franchise there. To determine the new team's name, Robbie held a newspaper write-in contest. The most popular choice among the more than 1,000 names submitted was "Dolphins." "It makes sense," Robbie explained. "The dolphin is one of the fastest and smartest creatures of the sea."

In the Dolphins' first season in 1966, speedy running back Joe Auer got Miami fans on their feet by returning the opening kickoff of the first game 95 yards for a touchdown. That was one of few exciting Dolphins performances, as the team struggled to a 3–11 record. Miami's first coach, George Wilson, had little talent with which to work.

Things began to change for the better in 1967 when Miami drafted quarterback Bob Griese out of Purdue University. Griese had great intelligence and superb instincts, and he combined those with a strong arm. Griese helped Miami improve by only one win in 1967, but his play gave fans hope. The Dolphins added balance to their offensive attack when they selected two running backs in the 1968 joint AFL-NFL Draft—a battering ram of a fullback named Larry Csonka and an equally powerful halfback named Jim Kiick. Csonka's bruising blocks and Kiick's quick feet gave Miami a formidable backfield, and the team improved to 5–8–1 in 1968.

When Miami slipped back to 3–10–1 in 1969, Wilson was fired. Although he had trouble getting wins, Wilson's enduring legacy would be his ability to stockpile elite talent. During his time in Miami, he signed many players who would become Dolphins stars, including running back Eugene "Mercury" Morris, guard Larry Little, and defensive back Dick Anderson. In addition, Wilson took a chance on undrafted defensive end Manny Fernandez in 1968 and traded for linebacker Nick Buoniconti in 1969. Both would later prove to be big-game playmakers.

The turning point for the Dolphins came in 1970 by way of two important moves. First, Miami boosted its offense by trading a first-round draft pick for dangerous receiver Paul Warfield. But it was the second move, luring coach Don Shula away from the Baltimore Colts, that really changed the Dolphins' fortunes. Shula made it clear that he expected to build a champion in Miami. "My goals are the same every year— to win the Super Bowl," he said. "And we'll do just that."

Shula quickly transformed the struggling Dolphins into a powerhouse. In 1970, as the AFL merged with the NFL, Miami put together its first winning record (10–4) and earned a playoff berth. Although the Dolphins lost a hard-fought battle with the Oakland Raiders, 21–14, it was clear that Miami was ready to win.

Garo's Gaffe

One of the most famous and bizarre plays in Dolphins lore came with two minutes remaining in the 1972 season. It was the fourth quarter of Super Bowl VII, and the Dolphins were protecting a 14–0 lead over the Washington Redskins. Coach Don Shula looked to ice the game with a field goal from Garo Yepremian, his accurate and reliable kicker. But after a low snap from the center, Washington blocked Yepremian's kick. Players from both teams scrambled for the loose ball, but Yepremian got there first and picked it up. In an attempt to keep the play alive, he tried to make a pass. Years later, he recalled, "I thought, 'Oh, I've thrown a pass before in practice. I'll throw it downfield.'" Instead, the ball rolled off his fingers awkwardly, and he batted it forward … right into the hands of Washington defensive back Mike Bass, who raced 49 yards for a Redskins touchdown. "I watched the whole thing on the sidelines, and I couldn't believe what I was seeing," Shula said. Fortunately for Yepremian, the Dolphins' famous "No-Name Defense" bailed him out by stopping Washington's final possession to preserve the perfect season.

GARO YEPREMIAN PROVED HE WAS NO QUARTERBACK IN SUPER BOWL VII

THE UNDEFEATED DOLPHINS USED TWO QUARTERBACKS, BOB GRIESE AND EARL MORRALL

14

I n 1971, after another 10-win season, Miami earned its first American Football Conference (AFC) East Division championship and met the Kansas City Chiefs in the playoffs. That game turned into a marathon contest that remains the longest game in NFL history at 82 minutes and 40 seconds. After the teams traded scores throughout regulation and went scoreless in a first overtime, Dolphins kicker Garo Yepremian booted a 37-yard field goal in the second overtime for a 27–24 win.

The "Fins" proved they were no fluke by shutting out the Colts 21–0 in the AFC Championship Game. Although Miami lost Super Bowl VI to the Dallas Cowboys two weeks later, the team was primed for greatness. In the locker room after the loss, Shula implored his players, "We have to dedicate ourselves to getting back to the Super Bowl next season and winning it."

Larry Csonka

RUNNING BACK / DOLPHINS SEASONS: 1968–74, 1979 / HEIGHT: 6-FOOT-3 / WEIGHT: 235 POUNDS

Known for his throwback playing style, Larry Csonka was a reliable workhorse on whom coach Don Shula could always count to get the tough yards. He was the kind of player who "preferred to shake a little dirt out of my helmet," as he once said. And although he was fast enough to run around defenders, he preferred running over them. But Csonka wasn't just a great ballcarrier. He was also a bruising fullback whose blocks created wide holes for halfbacks Jim Kiick and Mercury Morris. "My role is to make the power running game work," Csonka said. "It's not a spectacular strategy, but I've lived and breathed it, and I know it works." Csonka made headlines when he made a money grab and signed with the Memphis Southmen of the new World Football League in 1974. The league folded in 1975, and Csonka returned to the NFL the following year and played three seasons for the New York Giants. For his last season as a pro, Csonka came home to Miami in 1979 and finished his legendary career where he started it.

Garo's Gift

Although infamous for an awkward play in Super Bowl VII, Garo Yepremian was an accomplished kicker with one of the NFL's most remarkable stories. Born in 1944 on the island of Cyprus, Yepremian moved to London, England, when he was 16. There, he made neckties and played professional soccer. He then came to the United States, hoping to become a football placekicker. His soccer stint kept him from playing college ball, so he approached professional teams. Yepremian tried out for the Detroit Lions on a Thursday in 1966. Three days later, he kicked in the first live football game he'd ever seen. "I had no idea how to put my uniform on," he later said. That wasn't his only area of ignorance. When his coach said the team had lost the coin toss, Yepremian ran to midfield, looking for the "lost" coin. "I keek a touchdown!" he yelped after making an extra point in an early game. But there was no doubt about Yepremian's ability. Long field goals in two regular-season games preserved the Dolphins' 1972 undefeated season. A 2-time All-Pro, Yepremian scored 1,074 points during a 14-year career, and *Sports Illustrated* named him the best kicker of the 1970s.

GARO YEPREMIAN SPENT NINE SEASONS KICKING FOR THE DOLPHINS

Perfection and Innovation

Shula never asked his players for perfection, but that's exactly what he got in 1972. When Griese broke his leg in the season's fifth game, 38-year-old backup quarterback Earl Morrall stepped in. Csonka and Morris, meanwhile, took the offense on their shoulders as each player rushed for more than 1,000 yards—a pro football first for two teammates in the same season. While Morris scored a league-high 12 rushing touchdowns, Morrall rounded out the brilliant performance of the offensive trio as the league's top-rated quarterback.

Miami's defense was just as impressive. Nicknamed "The No-Name Defense" because of its shortage of star-caliber players, it allowed the fewest points of any NFL team in 1972. "The nickname doesn't bother us," said safety Jake Scott. "I don't care if people remember my name as long as we don't have any losses." Scott's

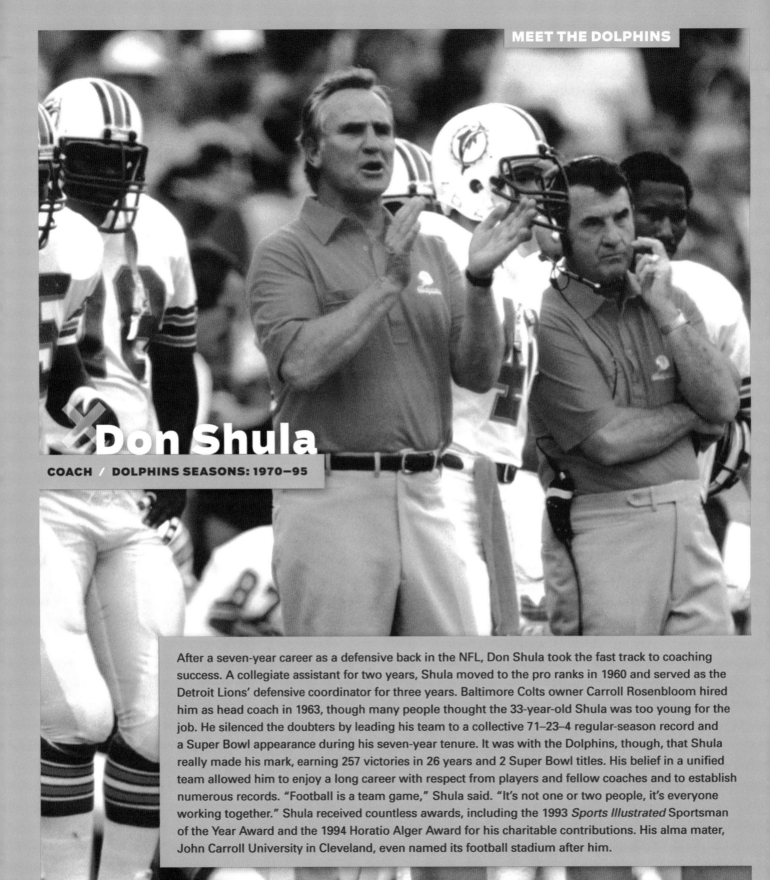

Don Shula

COACH / DOLPHINS SEASONS: 1970–95

After a seven-year career as a defensive back in the NFL, Don Shula took the fast track to coaching success. A collegiate assistant for two years, Shula moved to the pro ranks in 1960 and served as the Detroit Lions' defensive coordinator for three years. Baltimore Colts owner Carroll Rosenbloom hired him as head coach in 1963, though many people thought the 33-year-old Shula was too young for the job. He silenced the doubters by leading his team to a collective 71–23–4 regular-season record and a Super Bowl appearance during his seven-year tenure. It was with the Dolphins, though, that Shula really made his mark, earning 257 victories in 26 years and 2 Super Bowl titles. His belief in a unified team allowed him to enjoy a long career with respect from players and fellow coaches and to establish numerous records. "Football is a team game," Shula said. "It's not one or two people, it's everyone working together." Shula received countless awards, including the 1993 *Sports Illustrated* Sportsman of the Year Award and the 1994 Horatio Alger Award for his charitable contributions. His alma mater, John Carroll University in Cleveland, even named its football stadium after him.

"I don't care if people remember my name."

JAKE SCOTT ON THE
"NO-NAME DEFENSE"

words proved prophetic as Miami finished the regular season a perfect 14–0.

In the playoffs, Miami led the Cleveland Browns for more than three quarters. Cleveland jumped ahead 14–13 halfway through the fourth quarter, but the steely Morrall directed an 80-yard scoring drive to give Miami a 20–14 win. The next week against the Pittsburgh Steelers in the AFC Championship Game, however, Morrall struggled. After he threw an interception, Shula pulled him and barked to the now-healthy Griese, "Get us out of here with a win." Griese started the heroics with a 52-yard strike to Warfield, then Kiick scored 2 touchdowns to give Miami a 21–17 victory and its second Super Bowl berth.

Even though Miami was undefeated, most experts predicted that the Washington Redskins would win Super Bowl VII. But the Dolphins were determined to not have their perfect season ruined. The first quarter of the game was a defensive stalemate until Griese connected with receiver Howard Twilley for the game's first score. In the second quarter, Buoniconti snared an interception and returned it 32 yards. Soon after, Kiick plunged into the end zone to put Miami up 14–0 at halftime.

In the second half, the No-Namers rose up. On Washington's final offensive series, Manny Fernandez sacked quarterback Billy Kilmer for his 17th tackle of the game, then defensive ends Vern Den Herder and Bill Stanfill buried Kilmer on the series' final play. The Dolphins won their first world championship with the first—and still only—perfect season in NFL history. "No question, our approach to this Super Bowl was much different from that of the previous year," linebacker Doug Swift said. "In Super Bowl VI,

Butch Csonka and the Sundance Kiick

Dolphins running backs Larry Csonka and Jim Kiick wreaked havoc on the field. Off it, the best friends sometimes made even more noise with their pranks. In 1969, upon hearing of their exploits on and off the field, sportswriter Bill Braucher of the *Miami Herald* dubbed them "Butch Cassidy and the Sundance Kid," a reference to a 1969 movie about western outlaw buddies that starred Paul Newman and Robert Redford. In 1973, Csonka and Kiick wrote a book together, *Always on the Run*, with sportswriter Dave Anderson. In it, they discussed their childhoods, college football careers, and experiences in the pros. They also detailed their sometimes rocky relationship with coach Don Shula. Many players were afraid of the stern Shula, but "Butch and Sundance" loved to push his buttons. Csonka claimed to have once thrown a baby alligator in Shula's shower and later, a black rubber hose that he pretended was a snake, just to get a rise out of their coach. "I still don't know who is who," Csonka said in 2003. "We managed to get in a lot of trouble all the time with everyone, so that's probably why we got that title."

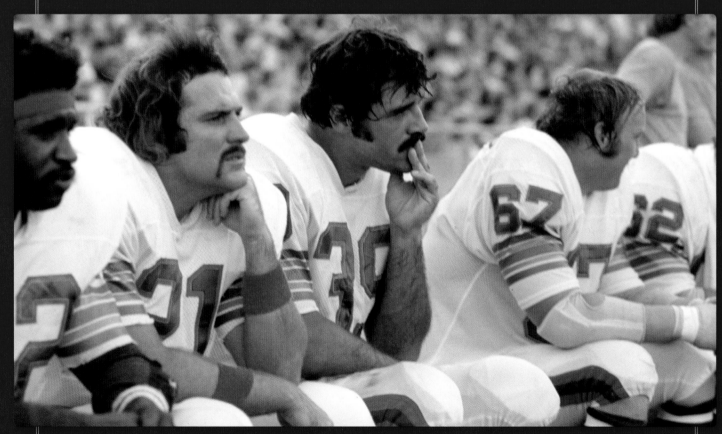

JIM KIICK (MIDDLE, LEFT) AND LARRY CSONKA (MIDDLE, RIGHT) ON THE DOLPHINS' BENCH

PAUL WARFIELD WAS ELECTED TO THE HALL OF FAME IN 1983

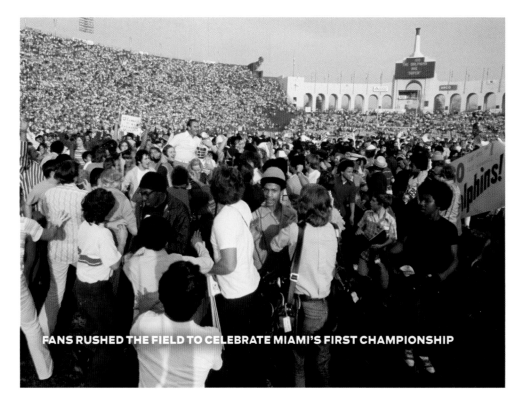

FANS RUSHED THE FIELD TO CELEBRATE MIAMI'S FIRST CHAMPIONSHIP

we didn't have our focus, but now we were intent on taking every play and every point seriously."

Elite teams always find a way to win. And the 1973 Dolphins seemed to find a different way to win each week. One game, cornerback Tim Foley was the hero, returning two blocked punts for touchdowns against the Colts. Then it was Warfield, who dominated the Detroit Lions by catching four touchdown passes.

Also that season, defensive coordinator Bill Arnsparger unveiled the "53 Defense," a scheme devised more out of necessity than innovation. Miami suffered a rash of injuries to its defensive line in the preseason. Forced to improvise, Arnsparger used linebacker Bob Matheson at defensive end but had him stand up like a linebacker. This gave Matheson the option of either rushing the passer or dropping back into coverage. The defense took its "53" name from Matheson's jersey number.

The Dolphins cruised to a 12–2 record, then crushed the Cincinnati Bengals 34–16 and the Raiders 27–10 to become the first team to advance to three straight Super Bowls. On Super Bowl Sunday, Csonka ran wild with 145 yards and 2 touchdowns to account for more than half of Miami's total offense, helping the Dolphins dismantle the Minnesota Vikings 24–7 for another world championship.

Miami won the AFC East in 1974 with an 11–3 record, but the Raiders proved that they were now an AFC heavyweight by narrowly beating the Dolphins 28–26 in the first round of the playoffs. That loss marked the end of a great era, as Csonka, Kiick, and Warfield all left town to play in the newly formed World Football League.

The No-Name Defense

In a scene from *Butch Cassidy and the Sundance Kid*, Butch looks back at a posse that has trailed them for a long time. "Who *are* those guys?" he asks. Dallas Cowboys coach Tom Landry said something similar before Super Bowl VI when reporters asked him about the stingy Dolphins defense, which had allowed just 174 points all year. "I can't recall their names," Landry said. That statement marked the birth of the "No-Name Defense." Although Miami lost that game, the No-Names were a key reason why the Dolphins won the next two Super Bowls and remained a perennial contender afterward. The group consisted of linemen Vern Den Herder, Manny Fernandez, Bob Heinz, and Bill Stanfill; linebackers Doug Swift, Nick Buoniconti, and Mike Kolen; and a secondary featuring Tim Foley, Curtis Johnson, Jake Scott, and Dick Anderson. Only Buoniconti was elected to the Hall of Fame, but defensive coordinator Bill Arnsparger thought they should be inducted as a group. "You can't single out one player," he said. "Nobody knew who they were, and they all played selflessly." Head coach Don Shula concurred. "The No-Name defense took a lot of pride in the 11-man concept."

OPPONENTS HAD TROUBLE MOVING THE BALL AGAINST THE "NO-NAME DEFENSE"

STAR QUARTERBACK DAN MARINO SPENT HIS ENTIRE CAREER WITH MIAMI

Marino and the Killer B's

Although Miami posted winning records in four of the next five seasons, it lost its playoff appearances in 1978 and 1979. Still, Miami's impressive air attack—featuring new star receiver Nat Moore—kept the Dolphins exciting. It had been a truly remarkable decade for the Dolphins. During the 1970s, Miami had put together a combined 104–39–1 record and brought two Lombardi Trophies to southern Florida as Super Bowl champions.

By 1980, Griese was starting to show his age and the wear and tear of numerous NFL seasons. New leaders began stepping forward to keep the Dolphins flying high. One of those new leaders was center Dwight Stephenson, an All-American from the University of Alabama. Hailed by coaching legend Paul "Bear" Bryant as "the best center I ever coached," Stephenson would be considered the NFL's premier center within a few seasons.

MUDDY DEFENDERS A. J. DUHE, BOB BAUMHOWER, AND DOUG BETTERS

Nick Buoniconti

LINEBACKER / DOLPHINS SEASONS: 1969–74, 1976 / HEIGHT: 5-FOOT-11 / WEIGHT: 220 POUNDS

During his solid career as a two-way player (guard and linebacker) at the University of Notre Dame, Nick Buoniconti was a natural leader who acted as the team's captain and was named an All-American his senior year. He carried those qualities into his split professional career—seven years with the Boston Patriots of the AFL and seven with the Dolphins. No matter what team he played for, Buoniconti was a star. Before the 1970 NFL-AFL merger, he played in six AFL All-Star Games, including one with the Dolphins. Considered by many scouts to be too small to play middle linebacker, Buoniconti was widely known as a guy who "played bigger than his size." The driving force behind the vaunted "No-Name Defense," he made a distinctive mark in Miami during the franchise's glory years with well-timed, game-changing plays that helped his team twice garner football's ultimate prize. He also inspired teammates with his outstanding play and fiery leadership. "Every play is like life or death," he once said. Buoniconti was so respected that his teammates named him the Dolphins' MVP three times.

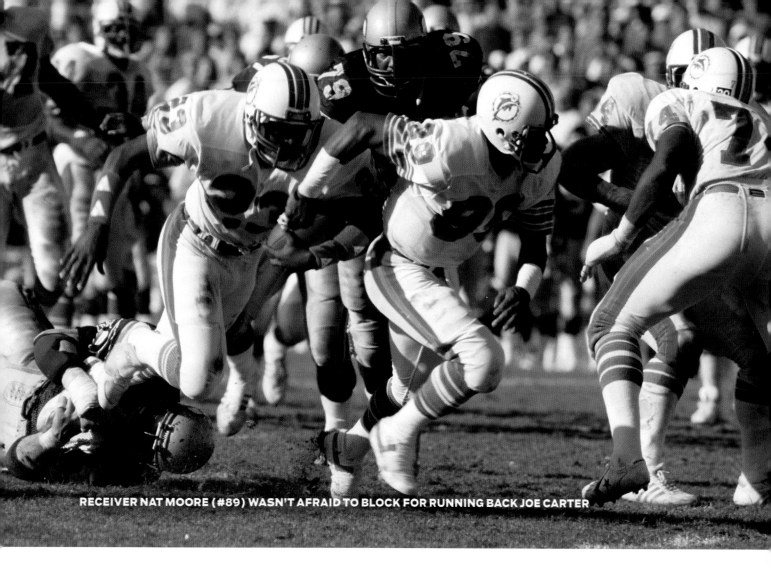

RECEIVER NAT MOORE (#89) WASN'T AFRAID TO BLOCK FOR RUNNING BACK JOE CARTER

In 1981, the fine play of Stephenson and nose tackle Bob Baumhower helped lead Miami back into the playoffs with an 11–4–1 record, but an overtime field goal by the San Diego Chargers ended Miami's season with a 41–38 loss. In a 1982 season shortened by a players' strike, Miami compiled a 7–2 record and convincingly thumped three playoff opponents (the Patriots, Chargers, and New York Jets), to earn its fourth Super Bowl appearance. Although the Redskins prevailed 27–17, Miami was revived.

In NFL circles, 1983 was called the "Year of the Quarterback." Five big-name signal-callers, including the Denver Broncos' John Elway and the Buffalo Bills' Jim Kelly, were drafted before Miami selected Dan Marino with the 27th pick. Although several quarterbacks from that draft would become stars, none would have the immediate impact that Marino had on the Dolphins.

"Dan the Man" was an NFL superstar as a rookie. In fact, at season's end, he would be the AFC's starter in the Pro Bowl. "You could tell right away that Danny had this unbelievable talent to throw the ball," said Moore. "He was so accurate … [and] had so much zip on the ball. For me, playing with Danny was more than anything like watching an artist at work. He could pick apart defenses no matter what."

Marino picked defenses apart at an even greater rate in 1984. By the ninth game, he had broken Bob Griese's team record for passing yards in a season. With the help of the sure-handed "Marks Brothers"—receivers Mark "Super" Duper and Mark Clayton—Marino finished the year with new NFL records in passing yards (5,084), completions (362), and touchdown passes (48). This gaudy performance earned him league Most Valuable Player (MVP) honors.

Assisted by the "Killer B's" defense (so called because eight players' last names began with the letter "B"), the 1984 Dolphins rolled to a stellar 14–2 record. Defensive linemen Doug Betters and Charles Bowser kept pressure on opposing quarterbacks, and Miami's offense overwhelmed the Seattle Seahawks and Pittsburgh Steelers in playoff wins to put Miami in its fifth Super Bowl, this time

RECEIVER MARK CLAYTON GRABBED 18 TOUCHDOWN PASSES IN 1984

WoodStrock

Between the end of Bob Griese's career in 1980 and the start of the Dan Marino era in 1983, Miami's quarterback was "WoodStrock." That was the nickname—which referred to the legendary 1969 multiday music festival in New York—that Miami media gave to the combination of David Woodley and Don Strock, who together bridged the gap between the two Hall-of-Famers. Each quarterback had his moments. During a playoff game against San Diego in 1981, a frustrated coach Don Shula put Strock into the game in the second quarter with the team down 24–0. Strock brought his team back in one of the epic games in NFL history, which the Chargers won 41–38 in overtime. Both Strock and San Diego quarterback Dan Fouts passed for more than 400 yards, 1 of just 7 times the feat has been accomplished in NFL history. Woodley had a near-perfect passer rating of 153.8 in the opening game of the 1982 playoffs as he led his team to the Super Bowl (in which he, at age 24, was the youngest-ever starting quarterback). Even though Woodley tossed an early 76-yard touchdown pass, the Washington Redskins defeated the Dolphins 27–17.

DAVID WOODLEY SPENT FOUR SEASONS IN MIAMI BEFORE GOING TO PITTSBURGH

DWIGHT STEPHENSON WAS A TRUSTWORTHY CENTER FOR EIGHT SEASONS

opposite the San Francisco 49ers. Marino boldly predicted victory, but the 49ers defense shut down the Dolphins' running game and stunned Miami 38–16.

The following year, Miami tied the Los Angeles Raiders for the best record in the AFC with a 12–4 mark. The highlight was a convincing 38–24 victory over Chicago, the only blot on the eventual world champion Bears' season. Miami fans hoped for a Super Bowl rematch between the two teams, but the Dolphins lost the AFC Championship Game to the Patriots. The defeat signaled the start of a late '80s slide, as Miami missed the postseason every year the rest of the decade.

In the early '90s, Miami reappeared in the playoff picture. After shutting out the Chargers 31–0 in a 1992 playoff game, the Dolphins committed five turnovers in an AFC Championship Game loss to the Bills. The biggest playoff heartbreaker came in 1994. After racing to a 21–6 lead over the Chargers, Miami was shut out after halftime and lost by one point, 22–21, missing a 48-yard field goal with only seconds remaining.

Despite that loss, 1994 was a special season for Coach Shula. Now in his 32nd year, he became the winningest coach in pro football history with a career regular-season record of 319–149–6. "His contributions to the NFL and the game of football extend far beyond his victory total," said NFL commissioner Paul Tagliabue. "Don Shula represents the highest standards of excellence by virtually any measure."

That same year, Florida businessman Wayne Huizenga bought the Dolphins from the Robbie family. The Dolphins went 9–7 in 1995 but were ousted by Buffalo in the opening round of the playoffs. Soon after that loss, Shula announced his retirement as coach.

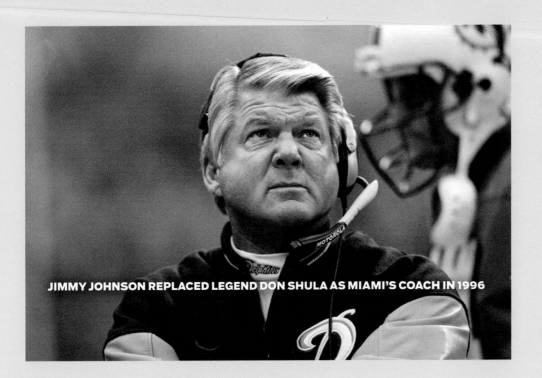

JIMMY JOHNSON REPLACED LEGEND DON SHULA AS MIAMI'S COACH IN 1996

Up-and-Down Dolphins

To fill Shula's shoes, Huizenga hired local legend Jimmy Johnson as the third coach in team history. Johnson had led the University of Miami to a national championship in 1987. He had also rebuilt the Dallas Cowboys from a 1–15 mess in 1989 to a Super Bowl champion in 1992 and 1993. Johnson made it clear that losing was unacceptable. "I expect results," he said, "and as long as I get results, I'll be a very happy person."

The Dolphins slowly improved in the late 1990s under Coach Johnson. He assembled a young, attacking defense that featured aggressive middle linebacker Zach Thomas, relentless defensive end Jason Taylor, and fast cornerback Sam Madison. On offense, the veteran Marino now slung the ball to speedy receiver O. J. McDuffie.

In 1998, Marino became the first NFL quarterback to throw 400 career touchdown

FEARED DEFENSIVE END JASON TAYLOR RACKED UP 131 SACKS IN MIAMI

✖Dan Marino

QUARTERBACK / DOLPHINS SEASONS: 1983–99 / HEIGHT: 6-FOOT-4 / WEIGHT: 218 POUNDS

Dan Marino always shared a close bond with his father. Affectionately known around their Pittsburgh neighborhood as "Big Dan," the elder Marino taught his talented son the unique throwing motion that helped young Dan become one of the NFL's all-time great quarterbacks. Most kids are taught to extend their arm when throwing. But Dan's father taught him to hold the ball next to his ear, then snap his wrist forward to get the ball out quickly. As young Dan practiced his technique on telephone poles and street signs, it became clear that he had a special arm. His signature throwing motion helped him set passing records in high school and at the University of Pittsburgh. It also earned him immediate success as a pro. Marino was selected to nine Pro Bowls, more than any other Dolphins player. His record-breaking 1984 season led the Dolphins to Super Bowl XIX. And by the time he retired in 1999, Marino had set nearly every NFL quarterback record in the books. When asked if he could always throw so well, Marino admitted, "You know what? Yeah. I could flat-out throw it."

passes. Yet despite his many passing records, Marino still lacked what he wanted most—a Super Bowl ring. He and all Miami fans were hopeful in 1999, when the Dolphins started out 7–1, but the team stumbled in the second half of the season. Although they beat the Seahawks 20–17 in the first round of the playoffs, their season came to a jarring halt the next week with a 62–7 loss to the Jacksonville Jaguars—Miami's worst defeat ever. Johnson resigned and was replaced by former Bears head coach Dave Wannstedt. Marino retired, bringing his amazing 17-season career to an end.

With a sturdy defense still intact, Wannstedt rebuilt the Dolphins' offense by adding veteran quarterback Jay Fiedler in 2000 and rookie wide receiver Chris Chambers in 2001. Then, in 2002, the Dolphins traded two first-round draft picks to the New

THE DOLPHINS PERFECTED THE "WILDCAT" OFFENSE WITH RONNIE BROWN

Orleans Saints for star running back Ricky Williams. Williams arrived in Miami with the ultimate package of skills—strength, speed, vision, and aggression. "We've had big guys and fast guys, but not the whole combination," said running backs coach Joel Collier. "Ricky's not a talkative guy, but his actions make things kind of fun around here."

The Dolphins' single-season rushing record of 1,258 yards, set by Delvin Williams in 1978, had stood for 25 years before Ricky Williams shredded it with an NFL-best 1,853 yards in his debut season wearing aqua and orange. With the defense bolstered by veteran linebacker Junior Seau, Miami went 10–6 in 2003, just missing the playoffs.

Then, in a shocking development, Williams—who had previously run into trouble with the NFL over drug use—announced his retirement before the start of training camp in 2004. The unfortunate turn of events left Miami again searching for an identity. At the end of that tumultuous 2004 season, Wannstedt was fired and replaced by Nick Saban, who had won the 2003 national collegiate championship at Louisiana State University. Saban lasted only two contentious seasons before leaving for another college coaching job. His replacement, Cam Cameron, oversaw a miserable 1–15 season in Miami in 2007 before being fired. Cameron's season was undercut by injuries, as quarterback Trent Green was hampered by a concussion and running back Ronnie Brown went down with a knee injury.

Desperate for a turnaround, Huizenga brought in former NFL coach Bill Parcells as executive vice president of football operations. "We talk a lot throughout this league, and Bill Parcells is one of those

A Historic Turnaround

Coming off a 1–15 season in 2007, the Dolphins sought improvement with a new coaching staff, led by Tony Sparano in his first head coaching job. After a 2–4 start in 2008, the team caught fire, winning 9 of its final 10 games. The only blot was a 48–28 beat down at the hands of the New England Patriots. The 11–5 mark represented a 10-game improvement, tying the 1999 Indianapolis Colts for the greatest one-year turnaround in NFL history. A key factor was the preseason signing of quarterback Chad Pennington, who had been released by the New York Jets after New York signed legendary signal-caller Brett Favre. Pennington led the league with a 67.4 completion percentage. His 97.4 passer rating was the league's second-best as he threw for more than 3,600 yards while posting 19 touchdowns and just 7 interceptions. Although Miami lost in the first round of the playoffs, Pennington's teammates appreciated his role in the exceptional season. "I should send a Christmas present to Brett Favre," said Miami wide receiver Greg Camarillo. "His coming out of retirement and going to the Jets is what allowed us to get Chad."

CHAD PENNINGTON WAS NFL COMEBACK PLAYER OF THE YEAR IN 2008

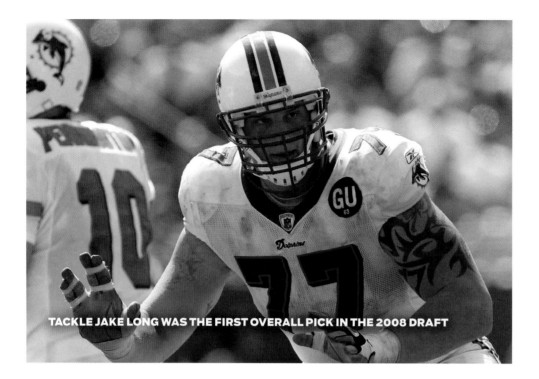

TACKLE JAKE LONG WAS THE FIRST OVERALL PICK IN THE 2008 DRAFT

names that if he comes in and he's on board, he's a guy that's going to get things going in the right direction," defensive tackle Vonnie Holliday said. Parcells quickly hired Cowboys assistant coach Tony Sparano as Miami's new coach and parted ways with longtime defensive stalwarts Zach Thomas and Jason Taylor.

The Dolphins began the 2008 season 2–4, then won 9 of their final 10 games to capture the AFC East title. The chief reason was the play of quarterback Chad Pennington, who joined the team after being released by the Jets. Pennington finished second in NFL MVP balloting after he threw for 3,653 yards and a league-leading 67.4 completion percentage. Unfortunately, the Baltimore Ravens ended the Fins' season in the first round of the playoffs, intercepting five Pennington passes.

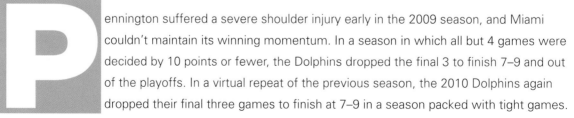

Pennington suffered a severe shoulder injury early in the 2009 season, and Miami couldn't maintain its winning momentum. In a season in which all but 4 games were decided by 10 points or fewer, the Dolphins dropped the final 3 to finish 7–9 and out of the playoffs. In a virtual repeat of the previous season, the 2010 Dolphins again dropped their final three games to finish at 7–9 in a season packed with tight games.

With a strong defense, the Dolphins looked to upgrade their offense in the 2011 NFL Draft. The club had high hopes for its top pick, center Mike Pouncey, whose twin brother Maurkice had made the 2010 Pro Bowl as a Pittsburgh Steelers rookie. Miami was also optimistic that second-round pick Daniel Thomas would be the power running back it had been seeking for several years.

Zach Thomas

LINEBACKER / DOLPHINS SEASONS: 1996–2007 / HEIGHT: 5-FOOT-11 / WEIGHT: 230 POUNDS

It is with good reason that Zach Thomas's favorite motto was "It's not the size of the dog in the fight, it's the size of the fight in the dog." Considered by many scouts to be undersized and too slow to play professionally, he answered critics by becoming the unquestioned leader of one of the NFL's most ferocious defenses in the late 1990s. "Coming into the league, I said, 'Just give me one year,'" Thomas recalled. Indeed, after starting every game but the opener as a rookie, he helped lead the Dolphins to five straight postseason appearances beginning in 1997. Thomas was the epitome of a fumble-inducing "run-stuffer." His secret was to get a quick jump on plays before his opponent knew what was coming. That instinct helped this on-field general set the Dolphins' team record for interceptions returned for touchdowns (4) and become 1 of only 3 NFL players ever to amass more than 100 tackles in each of his first 10 seasons. A 7-time Pro-Bowler with more than 1,500 career tackles, Thomas rightfully earned a place among the greatest defenders in Dolphins history.

REGGIE BUSH RESURRECTED HIS CAREER WHEN HE JOINED THE DOLPHINS

RYAN TANNEHILL WON SEVEN GAMES AS A ROOKIE QUARTERBACK IN 2012

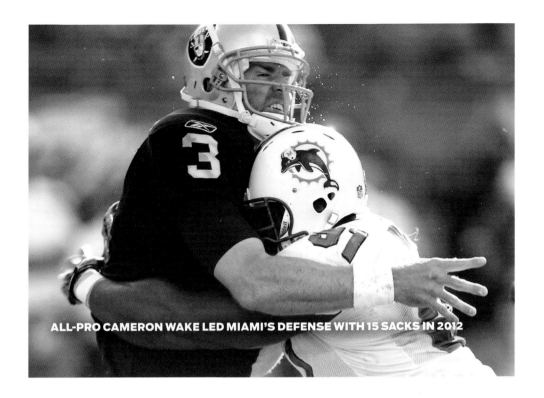

ALL-PRO CAMERON WAKE LED MIAMI'S DEFENSE WITH 15 SACKS IN 2012

But the Dolphins got off to a horrendous start in 2011, losing their first 7 games. They rallied to win 6 of their final 9, but it wasn't enough to save Coach Sparano's job. Sparano was fired, and the team hired Green Bay offensive coordinator Joe Philbin to replace him. "The Dolphins have a strong nucleus to build around, and working with everyone in the organization, I know that together we will return the team to its winning tradition," Philbin said.

Philbin wasn't quite as successful as he had hoped. Though the Dolphins were 4–3 at one point during the 2012 season and knocked off two eventual playoff contenders, they finished the campaign with a 7–9 mark for their fourth straight losing season. Still, there was reason for optimism. For the first time since 1983, Miami had taken a quarterback—Ryan Tannehill of Texas A&M University—in the first round of the NFL Draft. Tannehill started every 2012 game, and he broke four franchise records that had been set by Dan Marino as a rookie: passes attempted (484), passes completed (282), season passing yardage (3,294), and single-game passing yardage (431). Team owner Stephen Ross expressed his confidence in the young Tannehill. "I think we have our quarterback," he said. "What really impressed me is his intelligence and the type of person he is."

It has been a difficult decade for Miami—the franchise that still boasts the only perfect season in NFL history—as the Dolphins have earned just one playoff appearance since 2001. Yet fans in southern Florida remain confident that their team can turn the corner and regain the luster that characterized the franchise during its glory years. As Miami's franchise now nears its 50th anniversary, a new pod of Dolphins is aiming to swim back to the top of the NFL.